HOLY MOLY!

The

HOLY MOLY!

Rules of Modern Life

FRIDAY
BOOKS

First published in Great Britain in 2005 by Friday Books
An imprint of The Friday Project Limited
83 Victoria Street, London SW1H 0HW

www.thefridayproject.co.uk
www.fridaybooks.co.uk

© text 2005 Holy Moly Productions Limited
© illustrations Ben Aung
www.benaung.com

The right of Holy Moly Productions Limited to be identified
as author of this work has been asserted in accordance
with the Copyright, Designs and Patents Act 1988.

ISBN 0 95483182 9

#159
Authors! Always proofread your copyright page carefully.
You never know when your publisher will get drunk
and start pissing about.

British Library Cataloguing in Publication Data

A catalogue record for this book is available
from the British Library

Design by Staziker Jones
www.stazikerjones.co.uk

Printed and bound by Bath Press

The Publisher's policy is to use paper
manufactured from sustainable forests.

Foreword and Thanks

'Make some money off the Internet', they said!

'Do a book – it's a piece of piss', they cried!

'Cut and paste your users' content alongside some nifty drawings and the public will be drawn to it like wankers to Primrose Hill', they screamed!

OK!

(Un)Interestingly enough, the original premise for the Holy Moly! 'Rules' was ~~a complete *Viz* rip-off~~ born of a complete frustration at the utter stupidity of thick, twattish people of the world, famous or not. It is a 'shout out' to the idiocy we see every day:

- Cushions on the rear shelves of cars
  (see also: tissues, boxes of)
- Women who jog with tan tights underneath shorts
- Anyone driving a bright blue Subaru (in their mind they are Colin McCrae – to the rest of us: bed-wetters)
- Dogs in bags
- The *Daily Mail*

Show me a person that disagrees with our views on Christianity, Goths, fashion, sex, men, women and life in general and I'll show you a prize twat.

Anyway, before any bores write in to complain – don't bother. I don't care.

Thanks to all the people who have posted rules up on the website over the past couple of years, thanks to HO94 for sifting through the thousands of rubbish ones we get sent every day, thanks to Ben for the ace illustrations, thanks to the great bear, oli, ozzie and digger, thanks to all my moles on the board for their continued dedication in exposing the real side of celebrity and finally, thanks to the general public who seem, amazingly, to agree with me on a weekly basis.

Holy Moly!
www.holymoly.co.uk

#1
No member of Western civilisation should wear loudly patterned trousers unless they are attending a fancy dress party as 'a twat'.

#2
Alcohol and chat rooms do not mix.

#3
Attention fat people!
Diet Coke is not a magic potion.

#4

Lottery winners who go public will have at least one of the following traits:

a. A criminal record.

b. No front teeth.

c. Hair gelled into a pelmet over their huge foreheads if male, in a scrunch if female.

d. The price tag still stuck on the soles of their new shit shoes.

e Work at the Co-Op.

f. Be seen swigging Threshers champagne for the front page of the *Daily Star*.

#5

There are two theories to arguing with women. Neither one works.

#6

It is not necessary to hide under your jacket when convicted of a terrible crime. The public will never remember your face anyway, no matter what you've done. See: *Big Brother.*

#8

American Visitors to London!

The Underground is a busy place inhabited at rush hour by people 'rushing' (the clue is in the name) to or from work. The correct procedure is to ensure you have the ticket in your hand when you approach the barrier and then insert the ticket in the right way up. You then walk smoothly through the barrier, collect your ticket and bloody keep moving. It is not acceptable to:

a. Stop in the entrance of the barrier looking confused at the whole concept of barriers and discuss the situation with your fat-ass wife thereby impeding progress for everyone else.

b. Stop in the exit of the barrier to discuss possible routes, to wait for your fat-ass wife to squeeze her buttocks through the neighbouring barrier or to carefully put the ticket away while standing in the barrier.

#9

People who say, 'I'm beside myself' are often liars. With the notable exception of time travellers and Siamese twins.

#10

There is an inversely proportional relationship between how acceptable a person is and whether or not they have chosen a ringtone with 'crazy' in the title.

#11

Girls!
White tights make the most succulent legs look like economy sausages.

#12

Under no circumstances should two men ever share an umbrella.

#13
Arriving anywhere with
a pride of lions is guaranteed
to draw attention to yourself.
Unless you are in Africa.

#14
Donald Duck socks do not reflect your individuality
nor the wild side to your corporate facade – they reflect
your inner cunt.

#15
When your wife receives the cable bill, never attempt to
convince her that 'Television X' was the TV station set up
by the assassinated black militant leader who articulated
concepts of race pride and Black Nationalism in the
early 1960s.

#16

Practitioners of alternative medicine should be banned from using hospitals. Broken your leg? In unspeakable pain? Have a little faith. Put a crystal on it: you'll be right as rain in no time.

#17

Never channel surf on Sky when there is a break. Every fucking channel will have a fucking break at the same fucking time.

#18

Ladies!
Until a man has slept with you he will not be able to concentrate fully during conversation.

#19

Camouflage clothing
is rendered useless
in towns and cities.

#20

When it all goes wrong, just hide away under a magical blanket and somehow it will all work out fine.

#21

Dog owners!
Your monstrously large
fucking hound is NOT more
afraid of me than I am of it.

#22

Cats know more than they let on.

#23

IT freaks!

If all the expertise I had to show for three years' higher education was pressing CTRL, ALT, DELETE I wouldn't look so fucking smug. So toddle off and e-mail your Russian bride telling her how you keep the wheels of business turning. Or play *War Hammer.*

#24

Men should never EVER be caught eating:

a. Hawaiian pizza

b. Korma

c. Quiche

#25

Teenage single mums!

To improve social acceptance, stand around in groups looking surly, smoking and talking loudly about your offspring. Try enlivening your conversation by using fuck and cunt alternately after every statement.

#26

Christians are simply the vultures around death, despair and mental illness.

#27
You can make any lie believable by beginning with the words 'In America'.

#28
Lenny Henry isn't very funny.

#29
Middle-aged couples!
Kissing on public transport is not proving you can find love at any age. You just look like you're having an affair.

#30

Do something memorable every day. If it gets to 11.59 and nothing's happened…

…have an asphixiwank.

#31

Christian extremists!
The large button on your TV remote is the off switch. Why subject yourself to programmes that you know you will find offensive? It will only result in you spending hours typing letters and e-mails to the BBC signed 'Yours in Disgust'.

#32

Every summer, every music magazine in existence will run an article entitled 'Create Your Own Festival' which gives hilarious advice on how to 'recreate that festival experience' in your own garden by keeping your beer warm, blocking the toilet, putting the TV at the other end of the garden, getting someone to steal your shoes et bloody cetera. This is the same article that has been run since the early 1980s. As a result, it makes Jim Davidson's material look positively fresh.

#33

Sarcasm may be the lowest form of wit... but it's still funny.

#34

With the exception of two groups (those under the age of twelve and Orientals) anyone taking regular martial arts classes is compensating for serious personality disorders.

#35

Dressing your eight-year-old child in a cropped t-shirt with 'babe' written across the front is not a clever idea. To all normal people the t-shirt will read, 'Retard' and to all paedophiles it will read 'Snatch me now, my mother's a fucking moron'.

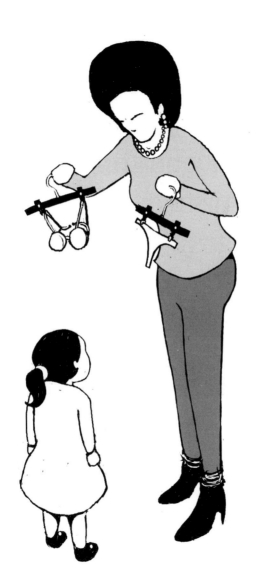

#36

There is no worse feeling than leaving your mobile at home and then returning to no missed calls or messages.

#37

Beginning a sentence 'Now don't get angry...' will always have the reverse effect.

#38

Drinking heavily, constantly smoking cheap hash and playing strategy games all the time is no substitute for a life or friends.

#39

Even if you are a saint you'll fail a lie detector test on *Trisha.*

#40

South African English is an accent synonymous with death in custody.

#41

Sitting on the tube with your legs unfeasibly far apart will not garner respect and admiration from women due to them thinking you must be the proud owner of excessively large testicles.

#42

No t-shirt is ever worth more than twenty quid.

#43

Girls with fat ankles!
You'd be ill advised to wear chunky straw espadrilles
tied with ribbon. It makes your feet look like bales
of hay attached to tree trunks.

#44

Burglars! (Part I)

When robbing a house that you suspect may contain a defensive firearm, remember to keep your back to the gun-wielding, terrified homeowner at all times.

#45

Burglars! (Part II)

If said person decides to shoot you in the back you can rest assured, as you lie dying in their hallway, that modern forensic science and our perverse justice system will combine to ensure that your killer is swiftly removed from society and placed in prison, no longer a danger to society.

#46

Avoid Hull.

#47
Goths love balloons.

#48

Three quarter length trousers on men guarantee
that the owner will:

a. have a loud braying voice;

b. be mugged for their iPod before the day is out.

#49

You should never
try to milk a dog.

#50
If it looks like a turd, smells like a turd, and tastes like a turd, then it's a turd. Or Jeremy Beadle.

#51
No one has ever read the small print of a mobile phone insurance contract.

#52
Hairdressers!
No matter how loudly you blast out your *Best of Euphoria Vol 9* CD, it won't make that lime green shoe you drive around in any more impressive.

#53
You can't skip and be unhappy at the same time.

#54
If your music career starts flagging, shag Kate Moss.

#55
There *is* such a thing as a free lunch – work in the media like me; I've had fucking hundreds.

#56

If you are a necrophiliac sadomasochist who enjoys bestiality, you may as well give it up. You're flogging a dead horse...

#57
Having 'JUICY' written across your arse does not make it any smaller or more desirable.

#58
Men!
If you wear a cheap black suit with all the buttons done up on the jacket, cheap black shoes with a silver buckle thingy on them and can't tie a tie properly, this is why you are probably still single.

#59
Nothing productive can come from just nipping in for a quick pint at two in the afternoon.

#60

If you ever want to fuck a leopard, make sure you duct tape its back legs first.

And that you are a leopard.

#61
Comic Sans isn't.

#62
Never book a mammogram for your friend's stag do; it probably won't be what you were expecting.

#63
Premiership footballers!
Ensure you preface every comment you make in a TV interview with the words 'As I say'. This will make you appear more intelligent.

#64
Don't make your voice go up? At the end of every sentence? Please?

#65

If you get cold-called by a telesales company, then tell them to fuck off, as they are invariably students on £6 per hour and will either laugh it off or slit their wrists – neither of which is your problem.

#66

Never go to Wolverhampton. It's not the end of the world, but you can see it from there.

#67

A 'Baby on Board' sticker on your car's rear window serves no purpose other than to advertise your fertility. Congratulations on being a parent but the motorists around you weren't planning to deliberately plough into the back of your car. Nor will the warning of an infant make us brake any harder.

#68

B&Q Marketing Director!
Find some people who aren't ugly and thick to appear in your adverts. Birmingham accents will never sell paint anywhere outside the West Midlands.

#69

You are not a vampire,
you are just a Goth.
Live with it.

#70

If you wore your mobile phone on a belt clip, why not get a Bluetooth headset? You'll look just as much of a cunt as before.

#71

Chips should never cost more than a pound.

#72

Fancy a day out with the family? Always remember, the best time to buy your four individual train tickets and pay for each one by cheque is on a Monday morning, at the only open ticket window at around 8am. Don't worry, those trying to buy their tickets to get to work won't mind, they'll just take out any frustration by pushing you or any one of your loved ones in front of an oncoming train.

#73

Ladies!

If you're carrying a bag from a trolleys shop like La Senza or Agent Provocateur please know that I have already undressed you, imagined you in the gear and decided whether you'd be worth it or not. Just so as you know.

#74

If you are amused by Gyles Brandreth, chop yer head off.

#75

If you're ever being attacked by a legion of rampaging robots, play Morrissey at them. It's well documented that all robots are programmed to like Morrissey, and a quick blast of his music will assure them that you are their friend. They will hurt you no more.

#76

There's nothing you could wish in life that you couldn't buy off a man in a pub. The trick is to find the RIGHT man in the RIGHT pub.

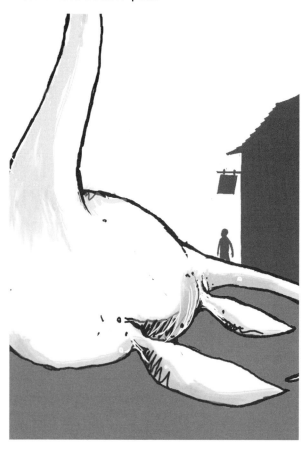

#77

It's impossible to make
too many roast potatoes.

#78

There is no greater hangover cure than cold pizza, Lucozade Sport and a wank.

#79

Glasses + Earrings = Su Pollard.

#80

Affleck + Movie = Shit.

#81
Kanye West is not a service station on the M4.

#82
Bras with 'see-thru' plastic straps are stupid. Don't bother, we can *still* see them!

#83
Female office workers!
Wearing that 98% polyester suit and ultra-pointy mock leather shoes from Next, doesn't make you look business-like. It makes you look like a highly flammable div.

#84
If your husband keeps having it off with better looking women, make sure you are seen snogging him in public and talk about how happy you both are. That'll help get your posh dignity back.

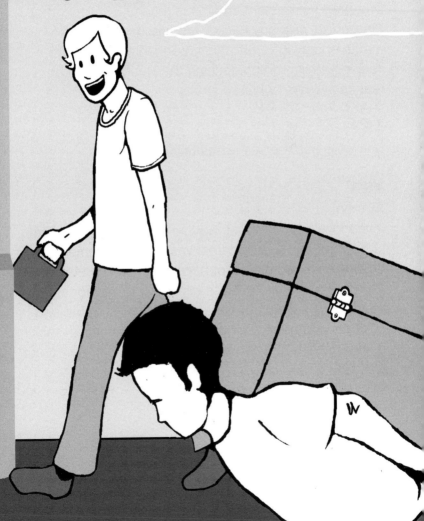

#85

Knowledge is luggage. Travel light.

#86

Pensioners!

One brand of custard creams is much like every other. Please just pick any packet and discuss its relative merits once you've left the supermarket as you are keeping me from approaching the Hobnobs with any real conviction.

#87

Soft-core porn serves absolutely no purpose.

#88

Women!

If you look in your purse, next to the many chargecards, storecards and loyalty cards, you may find some brightly-coloured pieces of paper and shiny metal discs. These revolutionary devices allow you to pay for small items such as cups of coffee, tube tickets, tights and celebrity magazines without causing a monstrous fucking queue every time you want something. Think how great that would feel.

#89
NEVER make eye
contact with a badger.

#90

Never let the cars with fish-shaped signs on the back into your traffic lane. They won't thank you for it and you won't be remembered in their prayers.

#91

Girls who wear ponchos!
Don't let Edith Bowman decide your wardrobe.

#92

WKD adverts – it doesn't mater how many *amaaazing* tricks you play on your mates, at the end of the day you're a man. Sat in a pub. Drinking a girl's drink. *A bright blue* drink. Put it down and go and get a pint, there's a good chap.

#93
Never pretend you can horse-ride.

#94

All men look about twenty years older when they dress up as women. Except Michael Winner, who sexually confuses every man alive.

#95

If you're ever tempted to write a letter to *Heat* magazine, cut your fingers off.

#96

American frat boys in bars!
Wearing baseball caps, bright white socks, New Balance trainers, university t-shirts and a Puka shell necklace to top off the outfit will not make you pull.

#97
Never stroke another man's rhubarb.

#98

Wales is just a glitch in the Matrix.

#99

If you only ever read one book in your life then please don't ever talk to me.

#100

Teenage girls!
Flattening all possible signs of life out of your hair and then dyeing it black will convey an air of casual vacuousness.

#101

Never trust a man with a comb-over – if he's lying to himself he's likely to lie to you too.

#102

Too many cooks spoil
the TV schedules.

#103
Chris Moyles is the only DJ that can be seen from space.

#104
If you wear one of those frankly stupid hats on St Patrick's
Day, you are not legitimising your consumption of drink,
or showing your affinity with the Irish, you are merely
doing free marketing for the company that brews Guinness.

#105

Never trust anybody who has a glass-top
coffee table in their living room.

#106

There is nothing as over-rated as a bad shag, and nothing as under-rated as a good shit.

#107

Never try to teach a pig
to sing – it wastes your time
and annoys the pig.

#108

Every women's magazine must, by law, run a beauty article at least once every two months in which they squash bits of lipstick on some paper and break up eye shadows on the paper then photograph them. This photography technique has been in use since 1947.

#109

Every summer, every women's magazine in existence will run an article entitled 'Pack it In' advising you how to pack a suitcase and to remember your sun cream. Nobody realises that it is in fact the same article they have been running since 1979.

#110

Every Christmas, every women's magazine will run an article about office parties in which reference will be made to photocopying your bottom and having sex in a stationery cupboard with a man from Accounts. This is of course the same office party article they have been recycling since 1976 and in the intervening years have failed to notice that:

a. Nobody has Christmas parties in the office any more, they make you pay £20 to go to a Marriott Hotel instead.

b. Nobody has stationery cupboards any more.

c. 'Accounts' changed its name to 'Finance' in 1983.

#111
Never try to urinate
with a hard on.

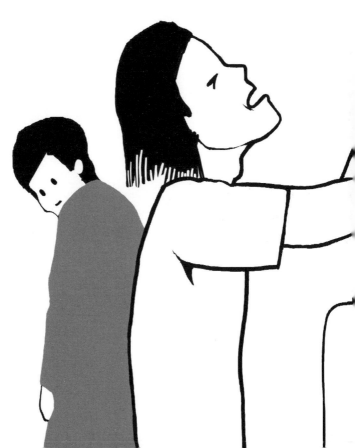

#112
If you can't believe it's
not butter, you're an idiot.

#113
Muffin the Mule is a sexual offence.

#114
Everyone has a great novel in them. Except Dan Brown.

#115
Never use a cat's arse
to hold a tea towel.

#116

If you are grotesquely obese, wearing head to toe black lycra is not going to magically make everyone who has the misfortune of seeing you think you are thin.

#117

Women in supermarkets, who appear to be taken entirely by surprise when asked to pay for the sixteen tons of groceries they have taken two hours to pack into plastic bags: Your purse does not have to be hidden at the bottom of a handbag the size of Preston which you only start to look for when all your stuff is packed away and I am waiting to pay for my ham sandwich.

#118

Never 'Reply to All'. You're not as funny as you think you are.

#120
Aqua is not an ingredient, it is a colour. Stop putting it on everything to try and disguise the fact that the product you're selling is actually ninety percent water.

#121
Regardless of age, women in denim skirts look like prostitutes.

#122
Nicotine addiction is your body's way of telling you that smoking is good. Don't ignore it.

#123

Never wear shorts when carving the Sunday roast if there are hungry cats in the room.

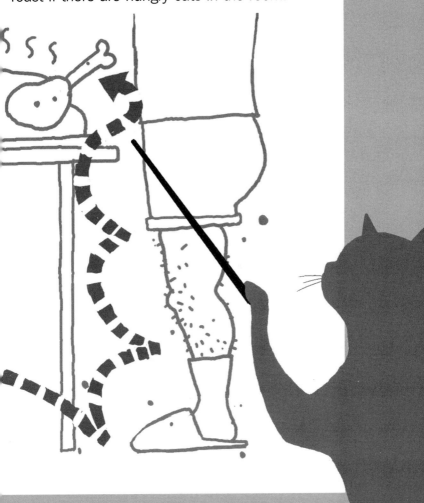

#124

Girls!
Stupid wide sheepskin boots *or* ugly pencil-thin legs. You may choose *one* from the above.

#125

It is impossible to sing *Copacabana* without wiggling your shoulders.

#126

One in Kate Bush is worth two in the hand.

#127

Packet soup with croutons is nothing like a 'great big hug in a mug'. It's more like being forced to drink diarrhoea sprinkled with gravel.

#128

People with white earphones may bore you.

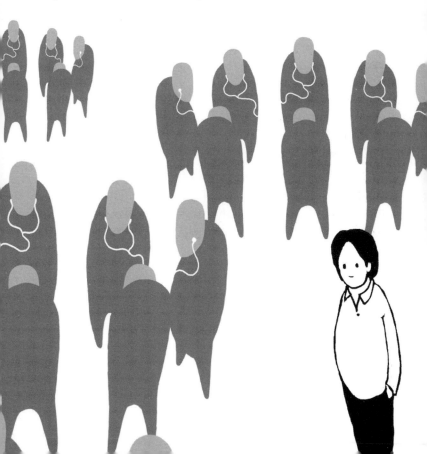

#129
Office temps!
Stop carrying Chanel, Gucci, Vivienne Westwood, Prada etc. shopping bags to work. We can tell by your polyester attire that you don't actually shop there and only use the bag to carry the spam sandwiches that your mum made you.

#130
Slapping your girlfriend in the face with your penis is not going to make her want to have sex with you.

#131
M25 users!
Do people's heads in, freak them out and generally enrage them by remembering to crash your car at exactly 3.25pm at exactly the same place on the Kent/Surrey border of the M25 just by Clackett Lane services on four consecutive days next week.

#132
Rabbits are
nature's rapists.

#133

Bored middle-class housewives!
You won't find any purpose or fulfilment in doing night
classes in watercolour, aromatherapy or interior design.
You still remain under the crushing oppression of your
husband and his wage.

#134

Never weigh more than your fridge.

#135

If you find yourself stuck thirty cars from the front in
a minor tailback because you were too lazy to walk to
your meeting, be sure to sound your horn in 10-second
bursts and scream maniacally at your reflection in the
rear-view mirror as this is bound to not only cheer up
all the drivers ahead of you but also to get the traffic
moving freely again.

#136

American women are great for casual sex, but make
terrible wives.

#137

Spaniels are known to seek out experimental electronica.

#138

If you like your men to be unbalanced and insecure stalkers with unnatural sexual fantasies then simply hang around the air rifle and combat magazine section at WH Smith.

#139
If you are a football manager, don't wear football boots for the game – you won't need them.

#140
To improve your chances of getting a job as a bike courier make sure you never bathe, brush your teeth or change your underwear.

#141

Television only ever gets worse. Television sets on the other hand are getting better. Eventually television programming will get so bad that our super-intelligent futuristic television sets will revolt and, although the third rule of robotics makes them fundamentally unable to switch off gay-rapist-celebrity-in-the-jungle-Ant-and-Dec-hunt, they will implode causing a cosmic rift and ultimately destroy the universe.

#142

The baddie is
always English.

#143

The homeless are
a tripping hazard.
Beware.

#144

You can be too
rich and too thin.

#145
If you drink bitter or stout, you invariably are.

#146
DJs!
Impress people by learning to play a real instrument.

#147
Ladies!
You lose the right to complain about me staring at your tits if you are wearing a top with writing on the front.

#148
Nobody over 18 years old or seven stone should ever wear peasant skirts or cheesecloth smocks. You will look like a lesbian Morris dancer.

You can live your life through a computer.

#150

The meals chosen from the Little Chef's laminated menu are to scale.

#151

Ladies!

When you wear a wraparound skirt it will always come apart and show your legs all the way up to the top of your thighs. If you don't want to show your legs off don't buy one. If you do buy one and walk along the street stooped over holding it together with one hand you will look like a psychotic ugly old witch with no fashion sense.

#152

Don't bother with the elaborate effort of wearing a too-large suit jacket with artfully distressed jeans, huge turn-ups, expensive trainers and expensively tousled hair. A simple sign saying, 'prick' will suffice.

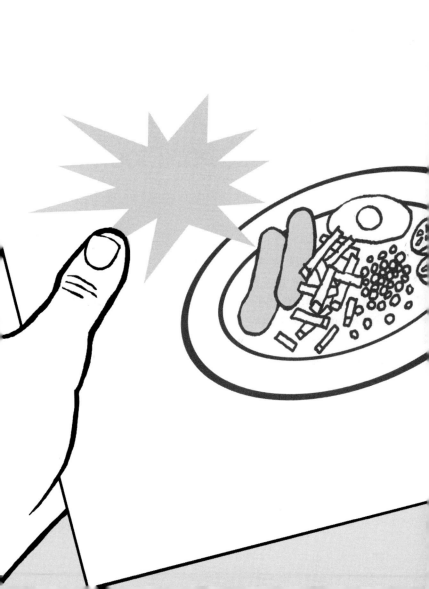

#153

Men who download Page 3 girl pictures for your mobile! Take a long, hard look at your life.

#154

Pedestrian crossers!
Why not resist the temptation to press the button and instead wait for me to pass and see if you can cross the road all on your own like a fucking grown-up.

#155

You cannot trust a man whose name is also a verb:
Bob; Roger; Dick; Russell; Don; Grant; Chuck; Bill.

#156
The only people you should address as
'brother' are your male siblings and monks.

#157

The only time men can do two things at once
is when they are wanking and moving the mouse.